Fabulous Meals in Minutes

Simply Dinner

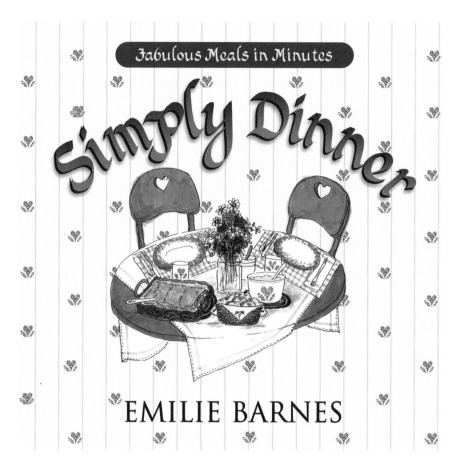

EMILIE BARNES

ILLUSTRATIONS BY CINDY GRUBB

Harvest House Publishers
Eugene, Oregon

Simply Dinner
Copyright © 1998 by Harvest House Publishers
Eugene, Oregon 97402

Library of Congress Cataloging-in Publication Data

Barnes, Emilie.
    Simply dinner / Emilie Barnes.
        p. cm.
    ISBN 1-56507-867-5
    1. Quick and easy cookery. 2. Dinners and dining. I. Title.
  TX833.5.B375 1998
641.5'4—dc21   98-14701
                                                      CIP

To obtain information about Emilie Barnes seminars, tapes, and other helpful time-management products, send a self-addressed, stamped envelope to:
    More Hours in My Day
    2838 Rumsey Drive
    Riverside, CA 92506

All works of art reproduced in this book are copyrighted by Cindy Grubb and may not be reproduced without the artist's permission. For information regarding art featured in this book, please contact:
    Grubbies' Inspirationals
    514 N. Union St.
    Ponca City, OK 74601
    (580) 765-8784

Design and production by Left Coast Design, Portland, Oregon.

Printed in The United States of America

98 99 00 01 02 03 04 05 06 07 / IP / 10 9 8 7 6 5 4 3 2 1

Fabulous Meals in Minutes

My mother always told me that a recipe book is worth the price you pay if only to find one recipe you like and use.

"Simply Dinner" will give you many meals that will provide you with cooking compliments. Family and guests alike will enjoy these simply delicious meals. Created for the busy household, each recipe will be simple, yummy, fun, and exciting to serve.

Your kitchen will be stress-less as you create a lovely meal—that is simply wonderful!

Enjoy!

Emilie

Sour Cream Cheese Enchiladas
Serves 4-6

Our 10-year-old grandson Bevan makes these for his family at least once a month.

INGREDIENTS

2	bunches green onions
1	pint (2 cups) sour cream
2	pounds longhorn cheddar cheese, grated
3	6 ounce cans enchilada sauce
20	8 inch flour tortillas
butter	

PREPARATION

Preheat oven to 350 degrees. Chop green onions, mix with sour cream. Leave out some onions for top of enchiladas. Warm enchilada sauce in medium saucepan on low. Mix half of the cheddar cheese with sour cream mixture. Butter tortillas and fry until soft, dip in warm sauce and fill with sour cream mixture. Fold enchiladas, place in baking dish, folded side down, and pour remaining sauce over enchiladas. Bake ½ hour at 350 degrees. Put remaining green onions and cheese on top 10 minutes before serving.

OPTIONAL

2 cups cooked chicken breasts, cubed

One Pot Pot Roast

INGREDIENTS

2 10½ ounce cans French onion soup
1 10½ can beef broth or consommé
2 to 3 pounds of pot roast
1 package baby carrots, about one pound

PREPARATION

Cut meat into one inch cubes and brown. Put the meat in slow cooker (crock pot); add carrots and rest of the ingredients to it. Cover and cook 6 to 8 hours on low or 4 hours on high. Serve with hot noodles or rice.

Takes 5-7 minutes to prepare!

*A man seldom thinks with more earnestness
of anything than he does his dinner.*

Samuel Johnson

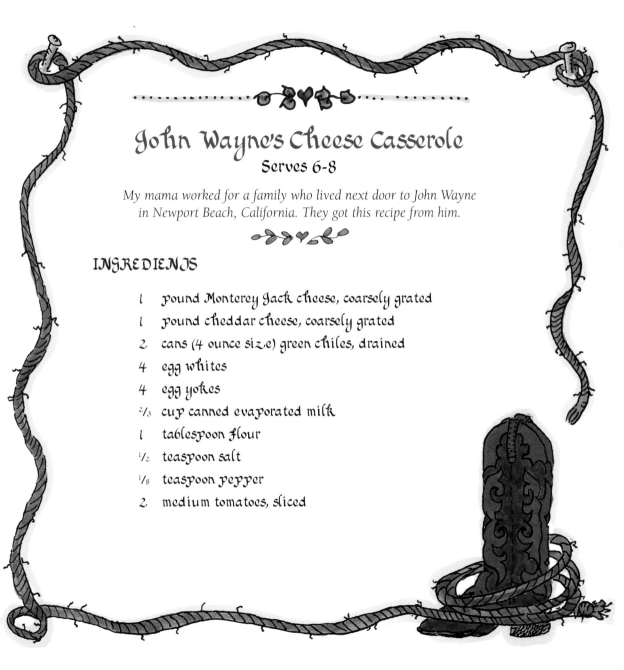

John Wayne's Cheese Casserole
Serves 6-8

My mama worked for a family who lived next door to John Wayne in Newport Beach, California. They got this recipe from him.

INGREDIENTS

1	pound Monterey Jack cheese, coarsely grated
1	pound cheddar cheese, coarsely grated
2	cans (4 ounce size) green chiles, drained
4	egg whites
4	egg yokes
2/3	cup canned evaporated milk
1	tablespoon flour
1/2	teaspoon salt
1/8	teaspoon pepper
2	medium tomatoes, sliced

PREPARATION

Preheat oven to 325 degrees. Remove seeds from chiles and dice. In a large bowl, combine the grated cheese and green chiles. Turn into well-buttered, shallow 2 quart casserole. In large bowl, with electric mixer at high speed, beat egg whites just until stiff peaks form when beater is slowly raised. In small bowl of electric mixer, combine egg yolks, milk, flour, salt, and pepper; mix until well blended. Using a rubber spatula, gently fold beaten whites into egg-yolk mixture. Pour egg mixture over cheese mixture in casserole, and using a fork, "ooze" it through the cheese. Bake 30 minutes; remove from oven, and arrange sliced tomatoes, overlapping, around edge of casserole. Bake 30 minutes longer, or until a knife inserted in center comes out clean. Garnish with a sprinkling of chopped green chiles, if desired.

OPTIONAL

You may use Ortega Green Salsa as a topping with the sliced tomatoes to further enhance this dish.

Southwestern Grilled Chicken
Serves 8-10

The total California patio meal!

INGREDIENTS

2 medium tomatoes, quartered	2 tablespoons fresh lime juice
2 cups onions, chopped	1½ teaspoons black pepper
½ cup red bell pepper, chopped	4 to 5 large whole chicken breasts,
4 garlic cloves	split, rib bones removed
¼ cup fresh cilantro leaves, packed	(boneless breasts can also be used)
⅔ cup soy sauce	parsley, freshly chopped for
6 tablespoons oil	garnish

PREPARATION

Place the tomatoes, onions, pepper, garlic, cilantro, soy sauce, oil, lime juice, and black pepper in a blender or food processor and blend for 30 seconds. Pour the marinade over the chicken breasts and marinate, covered and refrigerated, for at least 4 hours, turning frequently. Remove the chicken from the marinade and grill over medium coals for 20 to 30 minutes, turning frequently and basting with the marinade. Sprinkle the chicken with parsley before serving. Serve with California black beans.

I usually buy 2 cans of black beans and heat and garnish them with cilantro, or you can cook 2 cups black beans and follow the package directions.

Grape-Nut Casserole

*We were served this dish in Kosciusko, Mississippi, at the
home of our friends Joe and Dean Fenwick with a green salad and rolls.*

INGREDIENTS

2	chicken breasts
1	cup water
1	cup vermouth
1½	teaspoons salt
½	teaspoon curry
1	10½ ounce can mushroom soup
3	tablespoons mayonnaise
1	cup sour cream
½	pound mushrooms
2	boxes Uncle Ben's wild rice
1	cup Grape-Nuts cereal
½	cup butter
1	6 ounce package sliced almonds

PREPARATION

Combine chicken breasts, water, vermouth, salt, and curry, cook till tender. Debone chicken and soak in broth overnight. Strain broth and cook wild rice in broth, add water if needed. Sauté mushrooms in 1 tablespoon butter. Combine mushroom soup, mayonnaise, and sour cream with sautéd mushrooms. Cook at 350 degrees till bubbly and chicken juices run clear. For topping, sauté Grape-Nuts, butter, and almonds. Put over chicken, brown.

"Me is hungry," announced Teddy, who began to think that
with so much cooking going on it was about time
for somebody to eat something.

Louisa May Alcott
Little Women

11

Napa Valley Cheese Soup
Serves 6

*We serve this on a cold winter's day with crunchy bread and
Caesar salad, and we always get compliments!*

INGREDIENTS

1 cup potatoes, diced (optional)
4½ cups chicken stock
½ cup carrots, diced
½ cup celery, diced
½ cup zucchini, diced
2 tablespoons butter
2 tablespoons onion, finely chopped
½ cup flour

1 cup sharp cheddar cheese
¼ cup Parmesan cheese, grated
10 drops hot sauce
¼ teaspoon white pepper
½ cup dry white wine
1½ cups whipping cream
salt to taste
chopped parsley

PREPARATION

In a 2 quart saucepan add 1½ cups broth to carrots, potatoes, celery, and zucchini. Bring to a boil and simmer for 10 minutes. In 4-5 quart saucepan melt butter and add onion, sauté until transparent. Blend in flour and cook 5 to 7 minutes. Stirring constantly, be careful not to brown. Stir in remaining broth, slowly whisk over low heat until thickened. Add both cheeses and stir until melted. Season with hot sauce, salt, pepper, and wine. Stir in cream and serve; salt to taste and garnish with chopped parsley.

To make a good soup, the pot must only simmer, or "smile."

French Proverb

Meal Planning Made Easy

The average homemaker plans, shops, chops, pares, cooks, and cleans up for more than 750 meals a year! Keeping our families fed is a major part of our lives.

A few years ago, I found myself often serving as a short-order cook, trying to please everyone in the family. At any one breakfast I might fix French toast, waffles, scrambled eggs, pancakes, bacon, sausage, fruit, cold cereal, and oatmeal. By the time breakfast was over, I was ready to climb back into bed! Something needed to change before I lost my sanity.

I came upon a relatively simple solution: I decided to plan a week's worth of breakfasts, incorporating each family member's favorite breakfast one morning each week. On Monday, I might fix my son Brad's favorite, French toast; on Tuesday, my husband Bob's favorite, fried eggs over medium. I keep Sunday open for the cook's choice (or I let my husband cook that morning!).

It became such a pleasure to fix breakfast with this system that I very quickly expanded my planning to all our meals. And it motivated me to begin looking for new and interesting recipes and to scour the newspapers for money-saving sales. Now I always plan my meals an entire week ahead, check my cupboards and pantry to see what I have on hand, and make a marketing list for my trip to the grocery store. It saves me time and money.

Brother Ed's Fettucine with Zucchini and Mushrooms
Serves 6

My brother is a great cook!
He takes after our father Otto, the chef.

INGREDIENTS

1   16 ounce package fettucine noodles
      (I use spinach noodles if I can find them)
½ pound mushrooms
¾ cup butter
1¼ pounds zucchini
1   cup heavy cream
¾ cup Parmesan cheese, freshly grated
½ cup parsley

PREPARATION

In a large skillet sauté mushrooms sliced into ¼ cup butter over medium heat. Add zucchini, cut into julienne strips. Add cream and ½ cup butter, cut into pieces. Bring the liquid to a boil and simmer for 3 minutes. Cook noodles, drain and add to the skillet with fresh Parmesan cheese. Add parsley and toss with a wooden fork, gently combining mixture well. Transfer to a heated platter or large pasta bowl. Serve with additional fresh Parmesan cheese.

Roast Pork Loin
Serves 6-8

A great company meal—our guests always love it.

INGREDIENTS

2   teaspoons olive oil
1   tablespoon black pepper
1   teaspoon nutmeg
1   teaspoon cinnamon
3 to 4 pound boneless pork loin roast

PREPARATION

Blend oil, pepper, nutmeg, and cinnamon in small bowl. Rub mixture onto pork; cover completely. Place pork in shallow pan; roast in 350 degree oven for 1 to 1½ hours or until internal temperature is 155 degrees. Remove pork from oven; let stand 10 minutes before slicing.

Serve with rice, vegetables, and pineapple rings with cottage cheese on a bed of lettuce.

Salmon Fettucine
Serves 4

INGREDIENTS

1 small leek
1 small zucchini
1 tablespoon olive oil
salt and pepper
8 ounces heavy cream

3 ounces feta cheese
1 pound fettucine
4 to 6 ounces smoked salmon, thinly sliced
parsley, freshly chopped

PREPARATION

Dice the leek and zucchini and sauté in a frying pan with olive oil until golden brown. Add a bit of salt and pepper. Stir in cream and feta cheese, reduce sauce to the consistency you like. Cook the pasta as suggested on the package, drain. Stir into the saucepan, then serve. Joy with smoked salmon (rolled) and garnish with fresh parsley.

Serve with Caesar salad and Italian bread.

The Pasta Queen's Nicoise
Serves 4-6

Our daughter in-love, Maria, is the "Pasta Queen"—anytime I need pasta advice she comes to the rescue. This is a favorite Maria made for us.

INGREDIENTS

6 large, ripe tomatoes, seeded and chopped
4 cloves garlic, peeled and finely chopped
¼ cup capers, drained and rinsed
1½ cups black olives, pitted
⅓ cup loosely packed fresh oregano leaves, plus more for garnish
¼ cup flatleaf parsley leaves, torn
3 tablespoons extra-virgin olive oil
dash of balsamic vinegar
1 teaspoon salt
1 teaspoon freshly ground pepper
1 pound dry pasta, such as rigatoni, penne, rigate, or orecchiette
1 12 ounce can white tuna, drained well

PREPARATION

In a large bowl, combine all ingredients except pasta and tuna. Stir well, cover, and let sit for 1 hour. Set aside about 1½ cups. Cook pasta in boiling salted water until al dente. Drain well. Add to large bowl of sauce along with tuna, and combine. Serve in shallow bowls topped with some of the reserved sauce. Garnish with oregano.

OPTIONAL

Leftover grilled tuna or swordfish makes a delicious substitute for the canned tuna.

Barnes' Summer Salad
Serves 6-8

A MEAL IN ONE

Bob Hawkins, retired C.E.O of Harvest House Publishers, requests this meal every time he comes to dinner in our Barnes' Barn.

INGREDIENTS

All Chopped:
1 to 2 heads romaine le
2 large tomatoes
4 hard boiled eggs
4 cooked chic
1 pound bacon
1 bunch green o
1 cup blue chee
    cheese, my favorite
1 package mild Italian Good Seasons
    dressing mix made according to directions
1 16 ounce bottle ranch or blue cheese dressing

PREPARATION

Mix lettuce, tomatoes, eggs, chicken, bacon, onions, and cheese in large bowl. Toss with half of the Italian and half of the ranch dressing. Don't overload—just add enough to cover well.

Chili—The Low-Fat Way
Serves 6-8

This is a zesty chili I serve on a chili-winter's-day.
It hits the spot with hot buttered tortillas.

INGREDIENTS

> 1   medium onion, chopped
> ¼ cup chopped green pepper
> 4   cups water, divided
> 1   15 to 16 ounce can great northern beans,
>   rinsed and drained
> 1   6 ounce can salt-free tomato paste
> 1   14½ ounce can low-salt diced
>   tomatoes, undrained
> 2 to 4 teaspoons chili powder
> 1   teaspoon salt, optional
> ½ teaspoon pepper

PREPARATION

In a large saucepan,
cook the onion and
green pepper in ½ cup water
until tender. Add beans, tomato
paste, and tomatoes. Stir in chili powder,
salt if desired, pepper, and remaining water; bring to a boil.
Reduce heat, cover, and simmer for 20 minutes.

Foolproof Rib Roast

Yes, it does work. I do it often—well, 3 times a year!

1 standing rib roast, 4 pounds or more (depending on how many servings you need)

PREPARATION

Bring beef to room temperature. Place rib side down, on rack, in shallow roasting pan. Roast for 1 hour at 375 degrees. Turn off oven, but do not open door, leave roast in oven. Approximately an hour before dinner, turn oven on to 375 degrees and roast 30 minutes to an hour longer, depending on size of roast and degree of doneness desired (30 minutes for medium rare). Remove to hot platter and let stand 15 minutes before carving.

TIP

Start roast around 11:00 a.m. for dinner. For roast of more than 10 pounds, the final roasting time should be increased 1 hour. Use meat thermometer to check degree of doneness, as oven temperatures and room temperature of the meat can make a difference. 140 degrees = rare, 160 degrees = medium, and 170 degrees = well-done. Serve with steamed new potatoes, green beans, French bread, and crisp green salad.

Laughter is brightest where food is best.

Irish Proverb

Your Kitchen Essentials

No matter how large or small your kitchen is, you can tailor it to suit your style, if you give some thought to your cooking habits and needs. Start by taking inventory. Here are what I consider the essentials for every kitchen.

Pans

one 10" skillet with lid

one 8" to 10" omelet pan

a set of covered casserole dishes

1 roasting pan

2 bread pans

2 cookie sheets

1 double boiler

1 Dutch oven or similar type of pan

Basic Utensils

Start with a good set of knives and include a steel sharpener to keep your knives properly maintained.

1 set of measuring cups

a variety of wooden spoons

1 mallet (for tenderizing less expensive cuts of meat)

1 spatula

shears (great for cutting parsley, green onions, and meat)

1 rolling pin

storage bowls
1 vegetable cleaner
1 cheese slicer
tongs
1 garlic press

Gadgets

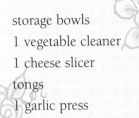

grater
colander
sifter
vegetable steamer
food grinder
eggbeater
whisk
egg slicer

Optional Larger Equipment

mixer
toaster oven
blender
food processor
wheat mill
microwave oven
an extra freezer

California Swiss Steak

INGREDIENTS

   1   package onion soup mix
   1   cup water
   1   cup wine
   1   10½ ounce can mushroom soup
   2 to 3 pounds swiss steak, browned in a Dutch oven

PREPARATION

Combine onion soup mix, water, wine, and mushroom soup. Pour over browned steak. Bake covered for 1 hour at 350 degrees, then uncover and bake 15 minutes more.

Hunger is the first course of a good dinner.

French Proverb

OTTO'S BRISKET

Otto's Brisket

*This was my father's brisket recipe.
He was a master chef trained in Europe.*

INGREDIENTS

1	2 to 4 pound brisket of beef
1	can beer
1	onion, quartered
3	garlic cloves, chopped
3	carrots, sliced
2	tablespoons sour cream
1½	teaspoons dijon mustard
2	teaspoons horseradish

PREPARATION

Put brisket in glass dish or oven pan. Add half of the beer, cover and cook 1 hour at 400 degrees. Add the other half of the beer, onion, garlic cloves, and carrots. Cover and continue to cook at 325 degrees 3 to 4 hours.

To make gravy, add to juices sour cream, dijon mustard, and horseradish.

Serve with sliced tomatoes and cucumbers sprinkled with red wine vinegar and olive oil; biscuits or corn bread; and/or roasted red potatoes.

Chad's Shrimp & Spaghetti
Serves 6

Our 13-year-old grandson, Chad, loves shrimp. He cooks this for all of us.

INGREDIENTS

    3 tablespoons extra-virgin olive oil
    2 cloves fresh garlic, pressed
    1 small onion, chopped
    1 pound shrimp (prawns), peeled
    ⅓ cup dry white cooking wine
    10 ounces ripe plum Roman tomatoes (egg shaped),
       peeled and chopped (or canned plum tomatoes,
       drained and chopped)
    salt and freshly ground pepper
    1 pound spaghetti
    1 tablespoon chopped fresh flat leaf (Italian) parsley

PREPARATION

In a large pot, bring 5 quarts salted water to a boil. In a large frying pan, heat olive oil over low heat, sauté garlic and onion until translucent, stirring frequently, about 3 minutes. Add shrimp, raise heat to medium, and cook, stirring constantly for 2 minutes. Add the wine and continue cooking until it evaporates, about 2 minutes. Add tomatoes and season to taste with salt and pepper. Cook for 2 more minutes.

Add spaghetti to the boiling water and cook until barely al dente.

Drain pasta and transfer it to the frying pan containing the tomato sauce. Add the parsley and cook over medium heat, stirring frequently, for 2 minutes.

Arrange the pasta on a warm platter and serve piping hot.

Serve with a fresh green salad, tossed with Italian dressing and garlic toast.

Sue's Sensational Parmesan Chicken
Serves 6

INGREDIENTS

1 cup soft bread crumbs
½ cup Parmesan cheese
¼ cup minced parsley
⅛ teaspoon salt
⅛ teaspoon garlic powder
½ cup butter, melted
2 pounds skinless, boneless chicken breasts
paprika

PREPARATION

Mix bread crumbs, Parmesan cheese, parsley, salt, and garlic powder.
Place butter in 9x13 inch dish. Coat chicken with butter, then dip
both sides of chicken in crumb mixture. Layer in pan with rest of
butter.

Garnish with paprika. Bake at 350 degrees for 1 hour. Baste twice
during baking. Cover with foil if chicken browns too much before it's
done.

Serve with brown rice, steamed broccoli, asparagus or green beans, and
sliced tomatoes.

California Chili Casserole
Serves 4

INGREDIENTS

1   3 ounce package cream cheese, at room temperature
¾ cup cottage cheese
½ cup sour cream
3   tablespoons green onion, minced
2   tablespoons green chiles, diced
¼ teaspoon salt
1   8 ounce can chili and beans
2   4 ounce cans ripe olives, sliced
2   cups corn chips
½ cup sharp Cheddar cheese, grated

PREPARATION

Preheat oven to 350 degrees. Blend cream cheese until smooth; add cottage cheese, sour cream, onion, green chiles, and salt; mix well. In a separate bowl, combine chili and beans with olives. Layer in buttered 1½ quart casserole dish, in order, 1 cup corn chips, cheese mixture, 1 cup corn chips, chili-olive mixture. Sprinkle top with more crushed chips.

Bake for 25 minutes. Remove from oven; sprinkle with cheese and bake 5 to 8 minutes longer or until cheese is melted.

You Won't Say Yuck, Because It's Yummy Tuna Casserole

Serves 4-6

INGREDIENTS

- 2 eggs
- 2 cups (1 pint) cottage cheese
  (You may use low-fat cottage cheese, if preferred)
- 1 6½ ounce can light tuna, drained and flaked
- ⅛ teaspoon pepper
- ½ teaspoon Worcestershire sauce
- 1 6 ounce bag of crushed potato chips
  (Lay's or Ruffles work well)

PREPARATION

Prepare water bath by placing large shallow pan of water in center of oven; preheat to 375 degrees. (Water should be deep enough to come halfway up side of 1 quart casserole.)

Beat eggs in large bowl, blend in cottage cheese, tuna, and remaining ingredients except chips. Pour into buttered 1 quart casserole and sprinkle with chips. Set in water bath and bake 35 minutes or until just set.

Planning the Perfect Kitchen

The key rule in organizing your kitchen is, "Things that work together are stored together." Take a few minutes to think through your daily work pattern and plan your space accordingly. For example, if you do a lot of baking, set up a baking center. It might be a countertop or a convenient cupboard or even a mobile worktable that can be rolled into your kitchen on baking day. Your mixer, baking pans, utensils, and canisters should all be readily accessible to this center.

Items seldom used, such as a turkey platter, deviled egg dish, roasting pan, seasonal tableware, and picnic gear, should be kept on higher shelves or stored in the garage on a special, easily accessible shelf. That will free space in your kitchen for the regularly used items.

Looking for some more ideas?

♥ Spices can be found quickly if stored in alphabetical order on a lazy Susan or a wooden spice rack on your wall.

♥ Use a crock to store utensils such as wooden spoons, whisks, meat mallet, ladles, and spatula on the stove. This can free up a drawer and allows for quick retrieval.

♥ If you get a new set of flatware, keep the old set to loan out when friends have buffets or church socials, or for family camping trips.

Once you've planned and organized your kitchen, you'll be amazed how much time you save and how much smoother mealtime preparation goes. And always be on the lookout for new and more efficient ways to store your equipment and food.

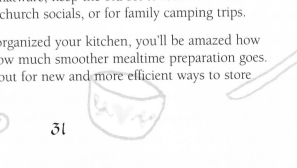

All-In-One Meal
Serves 8-10

INGREDIENTS

2 teaspoons salt
½ teaspoon pepper
1 teaspoon paprika
2 medium potatoes
1 cup celery
4 medium carrots
1 large green pepper

3 medium onions
2 pounds ground beef or ground turkey
1½ cups cottage cheese
   (You may use low-fat cottage cheese, if preferred)
1 16 ounce can stewed tomatoes

PREPARATION

Combine the seasonings; set aside. Peel and thinly slice potatoes; chop celery and carrots; mince green pepper; chop or slice and ring onions. Set all aside. Chunk hamburger into frying pan and brown. Drain excess fat and blend in cottage cheese.

In buttered 4 quart Dutch oven, layer the following in order, sprinkling seasonings over each: potatoes, celery and carrots, hamburger mixture, green pepper and onion; top with tomatoes and juice. Cover and bake at 350 degrees for 1½ hours. Uncover for last half hour.

Serve in individual soup bowls.

Fried Chicken with Garlic
Serves 4

My dad, the chef, used lots of garlic in his recipes

INGREDIENTS

Marinade:
- 1 cup sour cream
- 2 cloves garlic, crushed
- 1 tablespoon lemon juice
- 1 teaspoon Worcestershire sauce
- 1½ teaspoons seasoned salt
- ¼ teaspoon pepper
- 1 2½ pound frying chicken

Flour and cooking oil

PREPARATION

Blend marinade ingredients in medium bowl.

Cut chicken into serving pieces. Dip pieces in marinade to coat; put in refrigerator dish, spoon on remaining marinade, cover and refrigerate overnight.

Dredge marinated chicken pieces in flour and fry in hot cooking oil, 1 inch deep, until browned and crisp on both sides. Reduce heat and fry slowly until tender, about 40 minutes total. Do not crowd chicken in pan and do not cover.

This is home fried chicken at its best. And it's great with a veggie squash, biscuits, and mashed potatoes.

Chile Rellenos
Serves 8

INGREDIENTS

- 1   7 ounce can whole green chiles
- ½ pound Monterey Jack cheese, grated
- ½ pound cheddar cheese, grated
- 3   eggs
- 1   cup biscuit mix
- 3   cups milk
- seasoned salt

PREPARATION

Preheat your oven to 325 degrees.

Split the chiles, then rinse and remove seeds. Dry on a paper towel and arrange on the bottom of an 8½x11 inch baking dish. Sprinkle the grated cheeses evenly over the top of the chiles. Beat the eggs, then add the biscuit mix and milk and blend well.

Pour batter over the cheese and chile layer. Sprinkle with seasoned salt and bake for 50 to 55 minutes, until golden brown.

Serve hot. Joy with salsa for extra zing. For extra protein, add shredded, cooked chicken after the chili layer. Spanish rice and beans go great with this meal. You can top the beans and rice with some Monterey Jack and cheddar cheese.

Emilie's Orange Chicken
Serves 4

INGREDIENTS

- ½ cup butter
- ½ cup red currant jelly
- ¼ cup Worcestershire sauce
- 2 large cloves garlic, crushed
- 1 tablespoon dijon mustard
- 1 teaspoon powdered ginger
- 3 dashes Tabasco sauce
- 8 skinless chicken breast pieces
  or 1 whole chicken, skinned and quartered

PREPARATION

Combine butter, jelly, Worcestershire sauce, garlic, mustard, ginger, and Tabasco. Cook over medium/low heat till smooth. Cool sauce. Place in baking pan 1 whole chicken, skinned and quartered, or 8 skinless chicken breast pieces.

Preheat oven to 350 degrees.

Pour sauce over all; marinate in refrigerator for 2 to 3 hours, covered.

Cover chicken and bake for 1 hour. Uncover, increase temperature to 400 degrees and continue to bake, basting frequently until chicken is an even dark-brown.

Serve with rice pilaf and steamed zucchini.

Aunt Lisa's Chicken

This dish comes from Terra Torelli. It's simple and delicious!

INGREDIENTS

    4   skinless chicken breasts
    1½ sticks of butter (¾ cup), cold
    salt
    pepper
    Shilling's onion powder
    1   whole onion
    1   green bell pepper
    3   of your favorite kinds of cheeses, grated
        (approximately 2 cups of cheese)

PREPARATION

Preheat oven to 350 degrees.

Clean the chicken, then sprinkle with salt, pepper, and onion powder. (Do not overcoat with the seasonings.) After the chicken is seasoned, place it in a glass dish. Take 1¼ sticks of cold butter and cut it into chunks. Place the butter all around and on top of the seasoned chicken. Cover the dish with foil and bake for 1 hour.

While you are waiting for the chicken, chop the onion and bell pepper into small chunk pieces. Place the chopped pieces into a small skillet with remaining ¼ stick of butter and sauté until limp. Spoon over cooked chicken and sprinkle with cheese. Place in the oven until cheese melts, approximately 5 minutes.

This dinner is great served with baked potatoes, fresh green beans, and a nice green salad.

Chicken Cashew
Serves 4-6

INGREDIENTS

4 chicken breasts
½ cup flour
1 teaspoon salt
1 teaspoon pepper
⅓ cup olive oil

SAUCE:

1 13 ounce can pineapple chunks, in heavy syrup
1 cup sugar
2 tablespoons cornstarch
¾ cup cider vinegar
1 tablespoon soy sauce
¼ teaspoon ginger powder
1 chicken bouillon cube
1 large green pepper, very thinly sliced
¾ cup cashews

PREPARATION

Skin and bone the chicken, then cut into strips. Combine flour, salt, and pepper, coat chicken. Brown chicken in oil in a large skillet or wok. Place in a large baking dish and set aside. To make the sauce, drain the pineapple and reserve the juice. Add enough water to the juice to make 1½ cups liquid. In a saucepan, combine sugar, cornstarch, pineapple liquid, vinegar, soy sauce, ginger, and bouillon. Bring to a boil and cook for 2 minutes over medium heat, stirring constantly. Pour the sauce over the chicken and bake uncovered for 30 minutes in a 350 degree oven. Top with the pineapple, green pepper, and cashews and bake another 30 minutes. Serve over rice.

Em's Meatloaf

INGREDIENTS

1½ pounds lean ground beef or ground turkey
1 egg
½ cup onion, chopped
1 tablespoon chopped or pressed garlic, fresh
½ cup green pepper
¾ cup celery, finely chopped
¾ cup oatmeal
¾ cup low-fat milk or non-fat milk
½ cup catsup
1 teaspoon dry mustard
salt and pepper to taste
¼ cup wheat germ

PREPARATION

Combine all except wheat germ and shape into a loaf. Roll in wheat germ and bake 1 hour at 325 degrees.

I don't put my loaf in a loaf pan. I use a Pyrex dish. Sometimes I'll make 4 smaller loaves for individual servings. That way you don't have to slice, and they brown on all sides. Serve with baked potatoes and a vegetable.

Ground Turkey Noodle Bake
Serves 6-8

This casserole will be a family and potluck supper favorite.

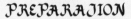

INGREDIENTS

- 1 8 ounce package medium or wide egg noodles
- 1 pound ground turkey
- 2 8 ounce cans tomato sauce
- 1 8 ounce package cream cheese,
     at room temperature
- 1 cup cottage cheese
- ¼ cup sour cream or
     low-fat sour cream
- ⅓ cup green onion, minced
- 1 tablespoon green pepper, minced

PREPARATION

Cook noodles according to package directions, add 1 tablespoon butter or oil to water; drain. Brown turkey in large frying pan, break into small pieces. Drain excess fat. Stir in tomato sauce and remove from heat. Blend cream cheese to smooth; blend in cottage cheese, sour cream, onion, and green pepper. Spread half the noodles over bottom of buttered 9x13 inch baking dish; cover with cheese mixture and then remaining noodles. Top with meat sauce. Bake at 350 degrees 20 to 25 minutes.

HAMBURGER NOODLES ITALIANO:

Sauté 1 clove crushed garlic with turkey. Add 1 teaspoon chili powder, ½ teaspoon basil, ½ teaspoon leaf oregano, and a pinch of ground cloves to meat sauce. Serve with shredded Parmesan cheese.

A Little Preparation

Preparing food as soon as it's brought home from the grocery store is a tremendous timesaver. No, I don't mean cook the food—just prepare it.

♥ If you already know how you will use your vegetables, they can be cleaned, cut or chopped, placed in plastic bags or Tupperware containers, and stored in the refrigerator—ready for salads, steamed vegetables, soups, or casseroles.

♥ Onions and green peppers can be chopped, placed in an airtight container or plastic bag, and frozen.

♥ A large block of cheese can be grated and frozen, allowing you to remove a portion whenever needed.

♥ Salad greens can be cleaned, drained, and stored for the week's salad. Remove the water from greens by putting them in a lingerie bag and placing them in the washing machine on the "spin" cycle for about two minutes. The greens will stay fresh and crisp for up to two weeks when stored in a plastic bag or plastic container in the refrigerator.

♥ Fruit prepared ahead of time will keep well if you squeeze lemon juice over it, toss, and refrigerate. The juice of half a lemon is enough for up to two quarts of cut fruit.

♥ Boil several eggs at once. They'll keep!

♥ Fry up ground beef and put into Tupperware. Freeze and it's ready for any dish.

♥ Fry the whole pound of bacon ahead, and take what you need for salads, B.L.T.'s, etc.

Tortilla Chip Casserole
Serves 6-8

Kids love these flavors!

INGREDIENTS

- 1 medium onion, finely chopped
- 2 tablespoons butter
- 2 8 ounce cans tomato sauce
- 1 4 ounce can green chiles, diced
- 2 teaspoons oregano
- 1 teaspoon salt
- 1 8 ounce package tortilla chips
- ½ pound Monterey Jack cheese, cut in ½ inch cubes
- 2 to 3 cups chunked, cooked chicken, skinned and boned
- 1 cup sour cream at room temperature
- ⅓ cup cheddar cheese, grated

PREPARATION

Sauté onion in butter until transparent. Add tomato sauce, chiles, oregano, and salt. Simmer, uncovered, for 10 minutes; remove from heat. Layer in buttered 2½ to 3 quart casserole, in order, half the following: tortilla chips, Jack cheese, chicken, and sauce. Repeat with remaining half of ingredients. Bake at 325 degrees 20 minutes. Remove from oven and spread sour cream over top; wreath with grated cheddar. Broil just until cheese melts. Serve immediately.

Gourmet Fillet of Sole
Serves 6

A party touch for fish fillets. A handsome buffet all-in-one main dish.

INGREDIENTS

1 6 ounce package white
    and wild rice mix
1 10 ounce package frozen asparagus
    spears or 1½ pounds fresh asparagus
1 cup celery, finely chopped
3 tablespoons butter
3 tablespoons flour
1 cup milk
½ teaspoon salt

1 teaspoon Worcestershire sauce
1 tablespoon fresh lemon juice
1 cup sour cream, at room
    temperature
½ teaspoon hot sauce
6 sole fillets (1½ to 2 pounds)
½ fresh lemon
2 tablespoons Parmesan cheese
2 tablespoons sliced almonds,
    lightly toasted

PREPARATION

Cook rice according to package directions, spoon into buttered 8½ x 11 inch baking dish. Cook asparagus according to package directions; drain. Meanwhile, sauté celery in butter. Stir in flour and cook 1 minute; add milk all at once and cook, stirring, until sauce thickens. Add salt, Worcestershire sauce, and lemon juice.

Empty sour cream into medium bowl, gradually add hot sauce, stirring constantly. Sprinkle fillets lightly with juice of half a lemon; salt to taste. Roll each fish fillet around 2 or 3 asparagus spears; arrange roll-ups on top of rice, lapped edge down. Spoon sour cream sauce over fish, sprinkle with cheese and almonds. Bake at 350 degrees for 25 minutes or just until fish becomes milky white and flakes easily.

It's good food not fine words that will keep me alive.
Wilson Mizner

Quick Burger Stroganoff
Serves 4

INGREDIENTS

- 1 medium onion, chopped
- 2 tablespoons cooking oil
- 1 pound lean ground beef or ground turkey
- 1 10½ ounce can cream of mushroom soup (you may use low-fat)
- 2 tablespoons catsup or chili sauce
- 1 small can sliced mushrooms, drained
- 1 cup sour cream, at room temperature
- salt

PREPARATION

Sauté onion in oil until transparent; add beef and cook until browned. Drain excess fat. Blend in soup, catsup, and sliced mushrooms; heat through. Remove from heat; add sour cream all at once and blend well. Heat gently to serving temperature. Salt to taste. Serve over hot noodles or rice. 4 ounces of dry noodles makes 2 to 3 hearty or 4 moderate servings.

The flickering of the blaze showed preparations for a cozy dinner…

Charles Dickens

Garlic Salmon Bake

INGREDIENTS

- 1 pound salmon
- ¼ cup olive oil
- 5 cloves garlic, mashed
- ¼ cup fresh parsley, minced
- 1 teaspoon basil
- ½ teaspoon salt
- ½ teaspoon pepper

PREPARATION

Spread olive oil over salmon in baking dish. Chop enough garlic to cover top of salmon. Put the fresh parsley over salmon and sprinkle with the spices. Bake at 350 degrees for 15 to 20 minutes, until salmon flakes easily.

Serve with fresh or frozen asparagus and buttered pasta sprinkled lightly with grated Parmesan cheese.

Boboli Pizza - Shrimp Style
Serves 8

*Seafood cocktail sauce adds a different taste to
a traditional food. This is also good as an hors d'oeuvre.*

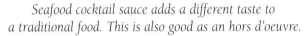

INGREDIENTS

1   16 ounce Boboli Italian bread shell
½ cup seafood cocktail sauce
4 ounces low-fat cheese (mozzarella or cheddar)
2 cups cooked shrimp (frozen works well)
thinly sliced green pepper, onions, mushrooms, and tomatoes

PREPARATION

Preheat oven to 450 degrees. Place Boboli on pizza pan. Spoon on
the cocktail sauce and add cheese. Arrange shrimp and vegetables
over cheese. Bake for 8 to 10 minutes or until cheese is melted.

Yoli's Budget Chicken Dinner
Serves 4-6

INGREDIENTS

- 1   10½ ounce can cream of celery soup
- 1   cup white wine
- ½   package Lipton Onion Soup Mix
- 2   bay leaves
- 6   chicken breasts (skinless, boneless-optional)

PREPARATION

Mix soup, wine, onion soup mix, and bay leaves. Poor mixture over chicken breasts and bake 1 hour at 350 degrees. Serve over white rice. Garnish with sliced almonds. "Herb Biscuits" (next page) are great with this.

Sit down and feed, and welcome to our table.

Shakespeare

Herb Biscuits

INGREDIENTS

1 package Pillsbury biscuits
1 cube butter, melted
½ teaspoon thyme
½ teaspoon sage
½ teaspoon garlic powder

PREPARATION

Cut each biscuit in quarters with scissors. Combine butter, thyme, sage, and garlic powder.

Dip each quarter in butter mixture.

Bake at 300 degrees until brown, about 12 to 20 minutes.

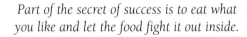

Part of the secret of success is to eat what
you like and let the food fight it out inside.

Mark Twain

Timesaving Tips

♥ Use the time when you're watching television for jobs like shelling nuts. Children often like to help in this task, especially if they can nibble while they help.

♥ Learn to do two things at once when working in the kitchen. I highly recommend a cordless phone (or a long extension cord) so you can reach every corner of the kitchen. While you're on the phone, you can…

> —load or unload the dishwasher
> —clean the refrigerator
> —cook a meal
> —mop the floor
> —clean under the kitchen sink

♥ Store food in a single layer to allow proper air circulation and to speed the freezing process.

♥ Before freezing fresh bagels, cut them in half. When you're ready to use them, they will defrost faster and can even be toasted while they are still frozen.

♥ Make up your shopping list according to your market. Go aisle by aisle so you don't have to backtrack.

♥ Don't shop when you're hungry. You'll fill your pantry with foods you don't have a clue what to do with.

Stuffed Pork Chops a la Yoli
Serves 4

Can't think of what to serve...this is it! I've served this to everyone.

INGREDIENTS

4 thick pork chops, have butcher slice with a pocket

STUFFING

- 2 cups cheddar cheese, grated
- 2 apples, chopped and cubed
- 2 cups bread crumbs
- 1 teaspoon cinnamon
- 1 cup orange juice
- 1 cup light raisins

SAUCE

- 2 cups maple syrup
- 1 cup white wine
- 1/3 cup grated fresh ginger root (purchase in the produce section of market)
- 1/3 cup soy sauce
- 1/2 cup flax seed oil

PREPARATION

Soak stuffing ingredients with orange juice. Mix all up and stuff into chops, close opening with toothpicks. Put into a square dish. Blend all sauce ingredients and pour over chops. Bake at 350 degrees, covered with foil for 1/2 hour and then uncovered for 1/2 hour. Serve with wild rice and baked tomatoes sprinkled with garlic powder and Parmesan cheese.

Quickie Spoon Bread

Our grandson, Chad, loves making spoon bread and asks to do it often.
He began making this recipe when he was nine years old.

INGREDIENTS

1 box Jiffy corn bread mix
2 cups creamed corn
1 small can green chiles, chopped
1 teaspoon sugar
1 egg

PREPARATION

Mix well and spoon into muffin pan lined with cupcake papers. Bake according to package directions.

Lemon Baked Salmon
Serves 4

Good for any fat fish such as bluefish, herring, mackerel,
pompano, whitefish, salmon, or mullet.

INGREDIENTS

2 pounds salmon steaks
1 tablespoon butter, unsalted
juice of ½ to 1 lemon
⅛ teaspoon salt (optional)
paprika
fresh minced or dried parsley flakes

PREPARATION

Place baking pan in oven with butter to melt. Lay steaks evenly in pan in melted butter and top with lemon juice, salt, paprika, and parsley. Bake uncovered at 350 degrees for 20 to 30 minutes, basting 1 or 2 times. Serve with tartar sauce.

Tartar Sauce

Blend thoroughly with wire whisk:
⅓ cup plain non-fat yogurt
1 tablespoon mayonnaise
1 tablespoon sweet pickle relish
1½ teaspoons lemon juice
½ teaspoon prepared
    mustard
⅛ teaspoon dill weed
⅛ teaspoon garlic powder

Emilie's Roast Lamb

*Our 14-year-old granddaughter, Christine, asked me for this recipe.
She loves leg of lamb served with brown rice and broccoli.*

1. Purchase a 5³/₄ to 6 pound leg of lamb.
2. Allow leg of lamb to stand at room temperature for 1 hour; peel and halve 6 cloves of garlic.
3. Wash and pat lamb dry; trim off excess fat layer, if desired, but not all of it.
4. Pierce lamb in several places about 1 inch deep with a knife and insert the garlic.
5. Squeeze juice of ½ lemon over top of lamb and sprinkle with remaining ingredients:
      garlic powder (generously)
      salt
      pepper
6. Insert meat thermometer in meatiest part of lamb and place on a rack over baking pan.
7. Place in preheated 325 degree oven and roast 35 minutes per pound or until meat thermometer registers 180 degrees.
8. Allow roast to cool 10 minutes before slicing. Trim all visible fat and slice.

Sweet and Sour Beans

Absolutely yummy, easy to prepare, and takes freezing especially well.
So low in fat that you can enjoy butter on the bread while keeping the
fat level low. Omit seasoned turkey for a vegetarian variation.

INGREDIENTS

1   pound ground turkey
½   teaspoon nutmeg
½   teaspoon sage
½   teaspoon thyme leaves
¹⁄₁₆ teaspoon cayenne pepper
2   medium onions, sliced and
        separated into rings
⅓   cup apple cider vinegar
¼   cup honey
1   teaspoon prepared mustard

1   teaspoon salt
2   15 ounce cans butter beans,
        drained and rinsed
2   15¼ ounce cans green lima beans,
        drained and rinsed
2   15¼ ounce cans red kidney beans,
        drained and rinsed
2   16 ounce cans Vegetarian
        Beans in Tomato Sauce (Heinz)
½   teaspoon garlic powder

PREPARATION

Blend turkey with seasonings and brown, remove from pan. Add onions to
the pan with a little water and cook covered until tender,
but not browned; drain off excess water. Add vinegar,
honey, mustard, and salt; simmer covered for 20
minutes. In large bowl combine onion mixture and
turkey with the beans and garlic powder.

OPTIONAL

Blend together and stir in, to taste:

¼   cup molasses
¼   cup catsup
1   teaspoon Worcestershire sauce

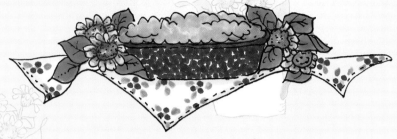

Favorite Tamale Pie
Serves 6

As a young bride I was asked to bring tamale pie to a potluck for Bob's staff at school. I had never made nor tasted a tamale pie in my life! Forty-five years later I'm still making it.

INGREDIENTS

1 pound ground turkey or beef
1 small onion, chopped
1 small green pepper, chopped
1/8 teaspoon garlic powder, or
    1 clove garlic, minced
2 cups tomato, spaghetti,
    or pasta sauce
10 ounces frozen corn
2 4 ounce cans sliced ripe olives, drained

1 1/2 teaspoons chili powder
1/2 teaspoon salt
1 cup cold water
1 cup cornmeal
1 cup water
1 tablespoon butter
1/2 teaspoon salt

PREPARATION

Brown together turkey, onion, green pepper, and garlic in large frying pan. Stir in sauce, corn, olives, chili powder, and salt. Simmer briefly and pour into 2 quart baking pan. Make cornmeal topping. Whisk cold water and cornmeal together until smooth in small mixing bowl; set aside. Place remaining cup of water, butter, and 1/2 teaspoon salt in saucepan and bring to boil. Whisk cornmeal mixture into boiling water; cook and stir over moderately low heat until thickened, about 2 minutes. Topping should not be runny. Spread hot cornmeal topping evenly and completely to the edges over top of pie filling. Bake uncovered at 350 degrees about 50 to 60 minutes or until crust is done (this timing can vary considerably depending on how thinly the batter is spread and how long it is cooked in the saucepan).

A feast is made for laughter . . .

The Book of Ecclesiastes

56

Company Chicken Tostadas

A real special occasion treat! We call them "Mexican Mountains" and have served them to over 50 football players and cheerleaders.

INGREDIENTS

    refried beans
    guacamole
    chicken, cooked and shred
    cheddar cheese, grated
    raw vegetables
    corn tortillas

PREPARATION

Before heating and assembling the tortillas, have all the ingredients prepared in desired amounts. Bake corn tortillas, 1 per serving. Place directly on oven rack, single layer, in a 350 degree oven for 10 to 12 minutes. Arrange over each crispy tortilla for individual servings in the following order:

    ⅓ to ½ cup refried beans
    1 cup shredded lettuce, mixed dark leafy and iceberg
    2 tablespoons to ¼ cup grated cheddar cheese
    ¼ cup to ½ cup shredded cooked chicken
    ¼ cup to ½ cup guacamole
    1 to 2 tablespoons yogurt/sour cream blend (half and half)
    5 cherry tomatoes or ½ tomato cut in wedges
    3 to 6 whole ripe olives
    sprigs of fresh parsley

The Perfect Pantry

Whether your pantry is a separate room or a couple of shelves in your cupboards, it's an essential element in organizing meals and saving money. I recommend that a pantry contain a supply of basic staple foods, including starches, sweets, condiments, and canned or bottled items.

Starches
* flour
* pasta
* cornmeal
* white and/or brown rice
* boxed cereal
* oatmeal
* a variety of potatoes

Sweet-based Staples
* honey
* maple syrup
* brown and white sugar
* jams and jellies
* apple juice

Condiments
* catsup
* brown and/or yellow mustard
* vinegar
* oil
* pickles
* olives
* capers
* salsa
* Worcestershire sauce
* canned tuna or any other canned fish or meat

Dried or Canned Fruits and Vegetables
* green beans
* tomatoes
* fruit cocktail
* applesauce
* raisins
* prunes
* variety of soups

Making the Most of Your Pantry

Here are a few helpful hints for making the most of your pantry:

♥ When stocking your pantry, organize your staples and canned goods in categories such as canned fruit, canned vegetables, meats, juices, cereals, etc.

♥ Keep an inventory of your pantry. Plan your menus using this list and shop only once a week, replenishing staples as necessary. Restock *before* you run out to avoid those "emergency" trips to the grocery store when unexpected company arrives.

♥ Place a colored dot on items you've purchased for a future recipe to warn your husband and children that these are not to be used for snacks.

♥ Investigate using a food service. It allows you to save time and money by shopping on the phone and ordering staples for six months at a time. This way your weekly shopping is limited to perishables, and often you can zip through the express line at the checkout counter.

Calico Beans

Ellen Cashman, our office manager, will bring a pot of these calico beans to our office for a yummy lunch on a cold, wintery day.

❦❦❧

INGREDIENTS

- 1 pound ground beef or ground turkey
- 1 pound bacon, cooked and drained (cut into 1 inch pieces)
- 1 medium onion, chopped
- 1 green pepper, chopped
- ½ cup brown sugar
- ½ cup catsup
- 1 16 ounce can kidney beans
- 1 16 ounce can lima beans
- 1 15 ounce can B&M baked beans
- 1 15 ounce can garbanzo beans
- 1 small can corn (optional)

PREPARATION

Brown meats, drain well, and mix together with all other ingredients except corn. Add corn before serving for additional color. Cook as a thick soup over medium/low heat. Also may be baked in a roaster covered with dollops of cornbread dough (bake according to cornbread directions).

This recipe is great in a crock pot, cooked all day on low...presto—dinner's ready! This makes a very thick full-bodied chili-type soup.

Dil's Baby Back Ribs or Chicken

Our dear family friend, Dil, comes to our home and makes this recipe for us as a special treat. We all eat, eat, and eat.

✦──⟡♥⟡──✦

INGREDIENTS

ribs or chicken
Lawry's 17 Seasonings
pepper
garlic salt
1 16 ounce bottle Newman's Own
    Italian Dressing
1 16 ounce bottle Knott's
    Honey Mustard Dressing
1 28 ounce bottle Bullseye
    Original BBQ Sauce
1 small bottle Kikoman
    Teriyaki Baste and Glaze

PREPARATION

Trim excess fat or skin from ribs, rinse under warm water. Sprinkle both sides with Lawry's 17 Seasonings, pepper, and garlic salt. Stir together Newman's Own Italian Dressing and Knott's Honey Mustard Dressing. Coat both side of meat and marinate at least 2 hours. I like to let it sit in the refrigerator overnight. Simmer on stove about 1 hour on low heat. The meat will start to pull away from the bone. Mix together Bullseye Original BBQ Sauce and Kikoman Teriyaki Baste and Glaze. Put meat on BBQ. Turn meat until light brown on both sides. Coat 1 side with BBQ mix. Let cook about 2 minutes. Turn and coat. Repeat this step until meat appears thick and gooey.

Lemon Herb Chicken
Serves 4

INGREDIENTS

1½ pounds chicken breasts, skinned and boneless

For marinade combine in a jar, cover tightly, and shake well:

>   juice of 2 lemons (about ½ cup)
>   ¼ teaspoon garlic powder
>   ¼ teaspoon thyme leaves
>   ¼ teaspoon marjoram leaves
>   ¼ teaspoon salt
>   ⅛ teaspoon rosemary leaves, crushed

PREPARATION

Pour marinade into shallow glass baking dish or pie plate. Arrange chicken in single layer in marinade. Cover and marinate in refrigerator at least 1 hour or in microwave oven on low for 6 minutes, turning pieces over halfway through. Bake uncovered at 350 degrees for 1 hour, basting with marinade every 20 minutes. If top of chicken reaches desired brownness before chicken is done, turn pieces over, or cover with foil to complete baking. Garnish with paprika to serve.

Serve with wild rice, broccoli, orange slices.

Emilie's Noodle Bake

A really simple casserole to make. Make a very quick
meal by adding tossed salad and French bread.

INGREDIENTS

- 8 ounce package flat spinach noodles
- 4 quarts boiling water
- ¼ teaspoon salt
- 1 teaspoon oil
- ¼ teaspoon pepper
- 1 pound ground turkey
- 2 cups pasta or spaghetti sauce
- 1 pint (2 cups) cottage cheese (non-fat) or 1% or 2% low-fat cottage cheese

PREPARATION

To cook pasta, add noodles, salt, and oil to boiling water and cook until barely tender, 7 to 10 minutes; drain. Brown the turkey and combine with remaining ingredients. Stir in cooked noodles and place in casserole. To serve immediately, heat covered in oven at 350 degrees for about 30 minutes.

Texas Meatloaf

This recipe is from Great Grandma Gertie's kitchen. Born in Texas in 1914, she still makes it for our family and serves it with baked potatoes and canned green beans (I prefer fresh, however).

><del>>~♥~<</del>

INGREDIENTS

1½ pounds lean ground beef (or ¾ pound
    beef and ¾ pound turkey)
¼ pound Jimmy Dean Hot Sausage
3 cloves garlic, chopped
1 medium onion, chopped
1 green pepper, chopped
1 tablespoon A-1 sauce
¾ cup oatmeal
2 eggs, beaten
3 slices bread, soaked in milk
    (squeeze out milk)
1 12 ounce bottle Heinz Chili Sauce
    (I use about 10 ounces of it.)
salt and pepper to taste

PREPARATION

Mix well with hands. Form in two loaves and put in a 13x9 inch dish and bake at 350 degrees for about 1½ hours. Cool 15 minutes before slicing. I always put the rest of the chili sauce on top to make it look pretty.

Perfect Peeling

Four quick and easy ways to peel:

❤ Cut off the bottom of an onion, then the top. Cut a slash in the side and remove the first outer peel, including the skin.

❤ Turn a fork-held tomato over a gas burner until the skin begins to darken and blister. It will peel right off.

❤ Place tomatoes in boiling water and remove pan from heat. Let sit for one minute. Remove the tomatoes from the pan, plunge them into cold water, and strip off the skins.

❤ With the palm of your hand, crush the entire head of garlic so that the cloves fall apart. Select one clove and place the flat side of a large knife over it; hit the knife gently with your hand. The clove skin will come off immediately. To get the smell of garlic off your hands, rub them in used coffee grounds.

Judy Brixey's Beef Casserole
Serves 6-10

Better known as "Train Wreck" by our kids, this recipe can usually be made from whatever is on hand in the fridge or the pantry.

INGREDIENTS

1 pound lean ground beef (or turkey) browned with
1 chopped onion and 2 to 3 cloves minced garlic.
Pour off any excess fat.

Pasta

Any type of pasta or rice that when cooked makes
about 3 cups.

Liquid

Either 1 28 ounce can chopped tomatoes including juice or
3 to 4 chopped fresh tomatoes plus 1 15 ounce can tomato sauce
or spaghetti sauce.

Crunch

1 cup chopped celery, microwaved for 4 minutes
2 cups cooked corn

OPTIONAL

> 1 cup sour cream
> 1 cup cheese, grated (maybe a combination of cheddar,
>   jack or Parmesan)
> black olives, chopped or sliced
> fresh basil leaves, torn
> parsley, chopped

Season to taste:

> salt, regular or seasoned
> pepper
> hot sauce to jazz it up

PREPARATION

You may add oregano or herbs de provence, or 1 to 2 tablespoons Worcestershire sauce. As you can see, there are endless variations and you can double the amounts indefinitely.

Bake covered in the oven for 40 minutes at 325-350 degrees, or you can simmer on low on the stove in a heavy bottomed pan with lid.

Spice a dish with love and it pleases every palate.

P l a u t u s

Broiled Game Hens with Apple-Thyme Glaze
Serves 2

INGREDIENTS

3 teaspoons olive oil
1 tablespoon minced onion
2 tablespoons apple jelly
1 teaspoon chopped thyme or ½
    teaspoon dried, crumbled
2 teaspoons cider vinegar
1 large Cornish game hen (about 1½ pounds),
    cut in half, backbone discarded
salt and pepper
apple slices (optional)
fresh thyme sprigs (optional)

PREPARATION

Preheat broiler. Heat 2 teaspoons oil in small heavy saucepan over low heat. Add onion and sauté until translucent, about 2 minutes. Add apple jelly and chopped thyme and stir until jelly melts. Mix in vinegar. Set glaze aside.

Rub hen halves with remaining teaspoon oil. Season with salt and pepper. Place hen halves skin side down in broiler pan. Broil about 5 inches from heat source until brown and crisp, 10 minutes. Brush glaze over. Turn hen halves over. Broil skin side up until just cooked through and juices from thigh run clear when pierced, 5 minutes. Brush skin with glaze and broil just until glaze begins to color, about 1 minute. Broil 15 minutes per pound; continue glazing and rotating.

Arrange hen halves on plates. Garnish with apple slices and thyme.

Accompany with baked winter squash and buttered, steamed cauliflower.

Vegetable-Smothered Chicken
Serves 4

INGREDIENTS

3 pounds chicken, skinned and cut up
³/₄ cup sherry or white wine
arrowroot or flour
3 tablespoons butter or olive oil
1 onion, chopped
4 carrots, cut in thirds crosswise
½ pound fresh mushrooms
4 green onions, sliced
¼ teaspoon red pepper
½ teaspoon garlic powder
1 teaspoon vegetable salt

PREPARATION

Marinate chicken in white wine at least 2 hours. Remove chicken and blot with paper towels, but reserve the marinade. Dredge chicken in arrowroot or flour; brown lightly in butter or oil and remove from pan. Add vegetables and seasonings, put lid on, and continue cooking until onion browns lightly. Return chicken to pan, add wine and simmer, covered, for 35 minutes or until chicken becomes tender.

Serve with orange muffins, rice, and a green vegetable.

Italian Zucchini Frittata
Serves 4

This is a good way to use zucchini in an omelet, and it's a delicious supper.

INGREDIENTS

- 4 cups zucchini (about 1½ pounds), unpeeled and grated
- 2 tablespoons onion, chopped
- ½ teaspoon garlic, chopped
- 4 eggs
- 2 tablespoons skim milk
- ½ teaspoon dried oregano
- ½ teaspoon dried basil
- ¼ teaspoon pepper
- ½ teaspoon salt (optional)
- 2 tablespoons Parmesan cheese

PREPARATION

Spray a 10 inch skillet with a non-stick coating. Sauté first three ingredients until zucchini is tender, pouring off any liquid. Meanwhile, mix eggs, milk, and seasonings (except cheese). Add to the zucchini mixture and cook until the eggs begin to set. Top with Parmesan cheese. Broil just until top is golden.

Serve with hot tortillas and butter.

Chicken Fajitas
Serves 4

INGREDIENTS

3   tablespoons lime juice
½   teaspoon coriander
½   teaspoon chili powder
1   pound boneless, skinless chicken
     breasts, cut into 1 inch strips
1   green pepper, sliced
1   onion, sliced
8   flour tortillas (6 inch size)
salsa (optional)

PREPARATION

Mix lime juice with coriander and chili powder and pour over chicken. Set aside. Meanwhile, slice vegetables. Add to chicken and mix well. Spray pan with non-stick coating and stir-fry chicken and vegetables until done. Warm tortillas in microwave about 50 seconds on high or in non-stick skillet. Fill each tortilla with chicken mixture and serve with salsa. This meal is great with black eyed beans.

Chicken and Rice, the Mexican Way
Serves 8

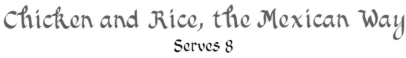

INGREDIENTS

- 1 medium onion, chopped
- 1 green pepper, chopped
- 1 teaspoon garlic, minced
- 1 16 ounce can canned tomatoes
- 1 4 ounce can chopped chiles
- 1 14½ ounce can chicken broth, fat removed
- 1¾ cups quick cooking brown rice
- 6 drops Tabasco sauce
- 2 pounds boneless, skinless chicken breasts
- 2 ounces cheddar cheese, grated

PREPARATION

Preheat oven to 350 degrees.

Cook onion and pepper in a skillet that has been sprayed with non-stick coating. Add next six ingredients. Mix well and bring to a boil. Remove from heat and spoon into a 9x13 inch baking pan that has been sprayed with non-stick coating. Arrange chicken on top of rice mixture. Bake, covered, for 35 minutes or until rice is done. Sprinkle cheese over chicken. Let stand, 5 minutes or until cheese is melted.

Making the Most of Leftovers

❤ Have some cooked meat left over, but not enough for an entire meal? Chop it up small, add a small amount of mayonnaise, bell pepper, celery, etc., and you have a great salad spread for sandwiches.

❤ Spread almost-stale bread with butter or margarine and sprinkle with grated cheese. Toast and top with a poached egg.

❤ When I have a few crumbs left in a bag of potato chips or box of crackers, I save them. After I lightly coat them with butter and toast them in the oven until brown, they make a tasty topping for casseroles or baked vegetables.

❤ For the two of us I bake six large potatoes. We eat them baked the first night. The second serving is sliced and fried in a bit of butter. The last two potatoes are cubed and served in a cream sauce with some cheese.

❤ Don't throw out the last cup of chili, beans, stew, or casserole—put it in a Tupperware container. At the end of the month, dump them all in a pot. Presto—a great surprise dish!

❤ Make homemade TV dinners from leftovers. Label them as follows: "Goulash/Date/Micro: High—one minute/Salad and Bread." By suggesting the cooking time and menu complement, you'll find that the leftovers are eaten, meals are rarely skipped, and money is saved.

❤ When serving leftover meat or fish, don't just reheat it. Prepare it in a different form. For example, grind it and shape it into patties, dice it for casseroles, or slice it thin and add to stir-fry dishes or to a white sauce.

❤ Turn your no-longer-fresh bread and crackers into crumbs for use in stuffings, casseroles, and meat loaf. Just put them in the blender, turn it on, and count to three. Then put the crumbs in a plastic bag for storage.

❤ Leftover orange, lemon, or lime rinds are great garbage disposal deodorizers.

Sweet and Sour Chicken
Serves 5

Serve this recipe over rice or noodles.

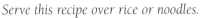

INGREDIENTS

1   8 ounce can unsweetened pineapple chunks, packed in juice
1   pound boneless, skinless chicken breasts
1   cup chicken broth (low-fat if you like)
¼   cup vinegar
¼   cup brown sugar
2   teaspoons soy sauce
½   teaspoon garlic, chopped
1   cup celery, sliced
1   small onion, quartered
1   green pepper, sliced
3   tablespoons cornstarch
¼   cup water

PREPARATION

Drain pineapple, reserving the juice. Cut chicken into bite-size pieces and place in a saucepan. Add reserved juice, broth, vinegar, brown sugar, soy sauce, and garlic. Cover and simmer over low heat for 15 minutes. Add vegetables and pineapple. Cook 10 minutes, stirring occasionally. Combine cornstarch and water. Gradually stir into hot mixture. Continue to cook until thickened, stirring constantly. Serve with quick-cooking brown rice.

Swiss Steak Italiano
Serves 6

Great Grandma Gertie Barnes made this for her family for over 60 years.

⊰⊱♥⊰⊱

INGREDIENTS

- ¼ cup flour
- 1 teaspoon salt
- 1 teaspoon pepper
- 2 pounds beef round steak, 1½ inches thick
- 2 tablespoons olive oil
- ¾ cup onions, diced
- ¾ cup celery, sliced
- ¾ cup carrots, sliced
- 1 15 ounce can Chef Boyardee spaghetti sauce with mushrooms

PREPARATION

Mix flour, salt, and pepper. Pound flour mixture into meat. Heat oil in skillet. Then add meat and brown well. Add spaghetti sauce, onions, celery, and carrots. Cook over low for 1½ hours. Cover skillet.

Give me neither poverty nor riches, but give me only my daily bread.

The Book of Proverbs

Saucy Spaghetti Squash
Serves 6

A delightfully different and meatless way to serve spaghetti.

INGREDIENTS

2 tablespoons olive oil
1 onion, chopped
2 cloves garlic, minced
1 medium carrot, chopped small
1 green pepper, chopped

1 cup fresh mushrooms, sliced,
    or 4 ounce can mushrooms
1 quart of spaghetti sauce
    (Ragu Homestyle is a good one)
1 medium spaghetti squash
    (4 pounds)

PREPARATION

To prepare sauce, sauté vegetables in oil, adding green pepper and mushrooms when onion and carrot are just tender. Add sauce and simmer 30 minutes to blend flavors. Meanwhile, to cook spaghetti squash, halve squash, remove seeds. Place half the squash cut side up in shallow dish, add 1/4 cup water, cover lightly with plastic wrap, and microwave for 7 to 8 minutes; let stand 5 minutes. Repeat with second half (or you may boil whole, covered with water 20 to 30 minutes; or bake at 400 degrees about 1 hour, then halve and remove seeds.

Run a fork around sides of cooked squash and pull out the spaghetti strings, place into a large mixing bowl.

Serve sauce over spaghetti squash, top with Parmesan cheese, if desired. It may be baked for 15 minutes at 350 degrees, if desired.

A Light Italian Pasta Deluxe
Serves 6-8

Some say this is a favorite recipe that actor James Garner cooks.

INGREDIENTS

olive oil
1   garlic clove, chopped
1   green pepper, chopped
1   small onion, chopped
½   pound ground steak or ground turkey
1   14½ ounce can whole tomatoes, drained
1   15 ounce can or 1 cup frozen corn
½   a 10¾ ounce can tomato soup
½   cup cheddar cheese, grated
½   teaspoon chili powder
¼   teaspoon cayenne pepper
salt and pepper to taste
¾   pound pasta, whatever kind you have on hand

PREPARATIONS

In hot oil, fry the garlic, green pepper, and onion until thoroughly cooked. Add ground sirloin, cook until browned. Add the tomatoes, corn, and tomato soup; mix well. Add grated cheese and stir until melted. Stir in chili powder, cayenne pepper, salt, and pepper to taste. Remove from heat and set aside.

Cook pasta according to package directions, drain. Add sauce, mix thoroughly, and place into a 2 quart casserole. Preheat the oven to 325 degrees. Bake uncovered, just until hot.

Eat-Every-Week Chicken Veggie Bake
Serves 4

This is a real favorite, especially with our grandchildren.

INGREDIENTS

1 3 to 4 pound chicken
3 tablespoons vegetable oil, divided
salt and pepper to taste
2 large onions, chopped
½ cup chicken broth or water
5 large potatoes, cubed
1 large green bell pepper, seeded and diced
5 large carrots, sliced
4 stalks celery, sliced

PREPARATION

Preheat the oven to 425 degrees.

Brush chicken with 1 tablespoon oil and sprinkle with a little salt and pepper. Place in a roasting pan, brown chicken for 20 minutes. Sauté the onions in remaining oil until nicely browned, stir in chicken broth or water. Arrange potatoes, green pepper, carrots, and celery around the chicken and pour browned onions over all. Sprinkle with a little pepper.

Cover and bake for 1½ hours at 350 degrees.

The browned onions enhance the flavor of the chicken and other vegetables. This is a great buffet dish, along with sweet pickles, fresh green salad, hot rolls, and pie.

Family Roasted Chicken

Serves 4

*Our daughter, Jenny, wins great compliments
from her family with this meal.*

INGREDIENTS

1 whole chicken (4 to 4½ pounds)
salt and freshly ground black pepper
1 cup water

¼ cup extra-virgin olive oil
¼ cup unsalted butter, at room
temperature

You can add red potatoes, carrots, and
celery if you like, right at the start, and have a meal-in-one!

PREPARATION

Preheat the oven to 475 degrees.

Place the chicken in a shallow baking dish. Sprinkle the chicken, inside
and out, with salt and pepper. Drizzle with the olive oil and dot with
butter. Place in the upper half of the oven and cook for 45 minutes,
basting every 7 minutes. Be sure to move the chicken around a bit to ensure
that it is not sticking to the dish.

After 45 minutes, turn off the oven. Leave the chicken in the oven for 10
minutes longer and then remove, let rest for 10 minutes.

Move the chicken to a platter; discard the fat in the baking dish. Add
the water to the baking dish and whisk well, scraping up all of the brown
bits on the bottom of the dish. Remove the sauce to a small saucepan.
Bring the sauce to a boil and cook for 3 minutes. Season with salt and
pepper to taste.

Carve the chicken, adding any carving juices to the sauce. Serve
immediately and pass the sauce in a gravy boat.

Lamb Stew
Serves 4

Growing up in a Jewish home,
I ate a lot of lamb—I still love lamb of all kinds.

INGREDIENTS

4 tablespoons olive oil
1 medium onion, chopped
2 cloves garlic, minced
1 pound lamb shoulder
 cut into 1 inch cubes
3 cups chicken broth

2 carrots, sliced
1 stalk celery, chopped
½ cup dry sherry
¼ teaspoon parsley, chopped
½ green onion, chopped
salt and pepper

PREPARATION

In a large pot, heat 2 tablespoons olive oil; sauté onion and garlic until translucent. Add the lamb shoulder and another 2 tablespoons olive oil. Sauté lamb until lightly browned. Add the chicken broth, carrots, celery, dry sherry, parsley, and green onion. Bring to boil, reduce heat, and simmer until lamb is tender, about 1 hour, skimming any foam from surface. Season to taste with salt and pepper.

Broccoli-Cheese Casserole

This dish from Sheri Torelli goes great with turkey, chicken, or just about any kind of meat.

INGREDIENTS

- 1 14 ounce bag frozen broccoli
  (thaw to room temperature)
- 1 can cream of chicken soup
- 1 small jar of Cheez Whiz (8 ounce)
- ⅓ cup butter, melted (or ⅔ stick)
- ½ cup onion, chopped
- 1 cup Minute Rice (uncooked)

PREPARATION

Sauté onions in butter; add to all other ingredients. Bake in a buttered 2 quart casserole dish for 30 to 40 minutes at 350 degrees. (You may microwave for 10 to 15 minutes in a microwave dish.) This recipe is very easy to double, triple, or whatever.

The cheerful heart has a continual feast.

The Book of Proverbs

Clever Tricks with Fruits and Vegetables

♥ Never store carrots with apples. Apples release a gas that gives carrots a bitter taste.

♥ Don't throw away a soup or stew that has turned out too salty. Instead, add a cut raw potato, and discard the potato slices when they are cooked. The potato will absorb most of the salt.

♥ When cooking vegetables in water, leave them whole. They'll retain more vitamins and minerals, and they're much easier to chop or slice after they're cooked.

♥ Slice raw tomatoes vertically so the inner pulp holds its shape for salads.

♥ Sautéed diced vegetables make a delicious low-calorie topping for pasta, baked potatoes, or rice.

♥ To get more juice out of a lemon, place it in your microwave on "high" for 30 seconds. Squeeze the lemon, and you will get twice as much juice— and the vitamins won't be lost.

♥ A great way to clean fresh mushrooms is to add three to four tablespoons of flour to a medium-size bowl of cold water. Wash the mushrooms in the water. The dirt adheres to the flour particles almost like magic. The mushrooms come out very clean.

♥ Never slice your onion to make soup. Just peel and put the whole onion in to make a sweeter pot.

Barbecue Chicken Pizza

My friend Marita Littauer Noon concocted this recipe at the request of her husband, Chuck. It's become a favorite of theirs.

INGREDIENTS

1   Boboli pizza crust, original
3   tablespoons olive oil (I use basil flavored olive oil)
barbecue sauce
1   red onion cut into 8 wedges, separated
1   red pepper, cut into ⅛ inch long strips
1   green pepper, cut into ⅛ inch long strips
2 to 3 boneless chicken breasts
1   cup cheddar cheese, grated
1   cup Monterey Jack cheese, grated
½ cup Parmesan cheese, freshly grated
1   4 ounce can olives, sliced

PREPARATION

Prepare barbecue, preheat oven to 400 degrees.

Place pizza crust on cookie sheet. Lightly brush crust with oil. Heavily brush with barbecue sauce. Set aside.

Brush chicken breasts with barbecue sauce. Grill for approximately 4 minutes per side or until cooked through.

Meanwhile, heat 1 tablespoon of olive oil in a large skillet over medium/ high heat. Add onion and peppers and sauté until soft and slightly browned, about 8 minutes.

Cut chicken crosswise into rough strips.

To assemble the pizza, sprinkle the cooked vegetables over crust. Evenly distribute the chicken pieces. Top with cheeses, then olives. Place in oven for 10 minutes, then slice and serve.

At feasts, remember that you are entertaining two guests, body and soul. What you give to the body, you presently lose; what you give to the soul you keep forever.
Epictetus

Southwestern Chicken Pasta
Serves 4

Another wonderful recipe from my friend Marita.

INGREDIENTS

3 tablespoons butter
2 large red bell peppers, cut into ¼ inch strips
3 garlic cloves, minced
¾ teaspoon cayenne pepper
3 to 4 chicken breasts, boneless
salt and pepper
12 ounces penne pasta
1 cup frozen peas
1 cup whipping cream
¾ cup chicken broth
¾ cup Parmesan cheese, freshly grated
¾ cup Monterey Jack cheese, grated
1 tablespoon basil

PREPARATION

Melt butter in large heavy skillet over medium heat. Add bell peppers, garlic, and cayenne; stir to blend. Cover skillet; cook until peppers are tender, stirring occasionally, about 8 minutes.

Meanwhile sprinkle chicken breasts with salt and pepper and grill until cooked through, about 4 minutes per side. Diagonally slice chicken and set aside.

Using a large pot, cook pasta according to package directions. Add peas during the last 5 minutes of cooking time. Drain. Return peas and pasta to pot.

Uncover skillet, add cream and broth and simmer until liquid is slightly thickened, about 5 minutes. Stir in $1/2$ cup of Parmesan cheese, $3/4$ cup grated Monterey Jack cheese, and basil. Remove from heat.

Gently blend bell pepper/sauce mixture and pasta. Place pasta on individual plates and top with sliced chicken and remaining Parmesan.

But come along; come into the kitchen.
There's a first-rate fire there,
and supper and everything.

Kenneth Grahame
The Wind in the Willows

Ground Turkey and Angel Hair Pasta with Tomato Cream Sauce
Serves 4

This is an extremely easy entree from Marita, suitable for a company dinner.

INGREDIENTS

1 teaspoon olive oil
1½ pounds ground turkey
1 cup green onions, sliced
2 14½ ounce cans diced peeled tomatoes
1 cup whipping cream
½ cup white wine
1 tablespoon tomato paste
1 16 ounce package angel hair pasta
Parmesan cheese, freshly grated

PREPARATION

Heat oil in a large skillet over medium heat. Add the turkey and green onions, sauté until cooked through, about 10 minutes. Stir frequently throughout cooking to break up the ground turkey. Add tomatoes with their liquid, cream, wine, and tomato paste. Simmer until sauce thickens, about 10 minutes.

Meanwhile, cook pasta according to package directions.

When sauce is ready, add the cooked pasta and toss until blended. Season to taste with salt and pepper. Place on individual plates, sprinkle with Parmesan cheese, and serve.

Small cheer and great welcome make a merry feast.

Shakespeare

Skinny Chicken a la Judy

My friend Judy Goyette has created a recipe that is virtually fat free.

INGREDIENTS

> 1 bag boneless, skinless chicken breasts
>   (Price Club, Sam's Club, etc.)
> celery salt
> paprika
> tarragon with lemon slices or chopped, dried garlic
> 1 cup chicken bouillon
> 2 tablespoons onion flakes
> 4 tablespoons white wine

PREPARATION

Preheat oven to 350 degrees. Rinse chicken breasts, and lightly salt both sides with celery salt while putting into large aluminum roasting pan. Paprika the tops (they will not brown). Sprinkle either tarragon or chopped garlic over the tops (add one slice of lemon to each breast when using tarragon).
For sauce, microwave bouillon and onion flakes for at least one minute before adding the white wine. Pour over chicken breasts and cover pan tightly. Bake for 25 minutes; uncover and continue baking for another 25 minutes. Serve immediately or cool and freeze.

Serve with rice pilaf, salad, and a veggie.

Chicken Fling
Serves 4

My friend Sheri Torelli got this recipe from her dear friend, Wilma Glidewell. It is very low in fat and delicious!

INGREDIENTS

- 1 whole chicken cut up (5 to 6 pieces) or 4 to 5 boneless, skinless chicken breasts
- 1 package Lipton Onion Soup Mix
- 1 10 ounce jar orange marmalade

PREPARATION

Use a 13x9 inch glass pan. Place chicken in the pan. Sprinkle onion soup mix over the chicken. Spread orange marmalade on top of the chicken and soup mix. Cover with aluminum foil and bake at 350 degrees for approximately 35 minutes.

"The Stuff"

*This buffet type meal-in-one from Janie Gaskins is
a crowd pleaser! It will serve large groups very easily.*

INGREDIENTS

Minute Rice (quantity depends on how many people you are going
    to serve)

canned chili (no beans)

fritos corn chips (crushed)

cheese, grated (cheddar, Jack,
    mozzarella)

sliced or chopped olives
    (drain excess juice)

peanuts, chopped

coconut, shredded

avocado, cut up in small chunks

tomatoes, chopped

lettuce, shredded

chopped green chiles

jalapenos

salsa

sour cream

Make a large pan each of Minute Rice (per directions) and chili.
All other ingredients are to be placed in separate bowls. Start with
rice, add some chili, and then use your creativity and personal taste
from there. Top off your plate with sour cream. You may add or
delete ingredients depending on your preferences. Serve with warm
flour tortillas and enjoy!

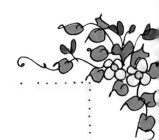

Donna Otto Pasta Gravy

INGREDIENTS

½ onion, chopped
1 clove garlic, chopped
3 tablespoons olive oil
2 6 ounce cans tomato paste
2 cups peeled tomatoes, mashed and blended
 in blender, or 1 16 ounce can tomatoes
6 cups water
1 teaspoon oregano
1 teaspoon basil
½ teaspoon whole fennel
1 tablespoon salt

PREPARATION

Brown onion and garlic in olive oil. Add cans of tomato paste. Sauté in oil and onion for 3 to 5 minutes over medium heat. Add peeled tomatoes and water. Stir well. Add oregano, basil, whole fennel, and salt. Simmer on low for 3 hours, stir well and often.

So simple it takes about 7 minutes to put together! I always double the recipe.

This gravy (Italians call it gravy because they put in on everything) will freeze wonderfully, and it does go over anything: pastas, vegetables, meat, and lasagna dishes.

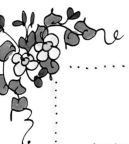
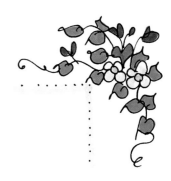

MENU

Loaf of sour dough bread, sliced and brushed with melted garlic butter. Brush each slice and across the top, wrap in foil keeping the top open so the bread is soft in the center...crunchy on top.

Tossed salad with wine vinegar and olive oil dressing.

Pasta, any kind. Our favorites are capelini and mostaccoli.

Gravy (see previous page)

Fresh grated Romano cheese

DESSERT

1 3 ounce package strawberry Jell-O, jelled; 2 cups of vanilla ice cream, and fresh strawberries. Put ice cream and Jell-O in mixing bowl and beat at medium speed until blended. Pour into individual dessert dishes...top with fresh berries.

The entire meal is done in advance...so you can be available to your family and friends.

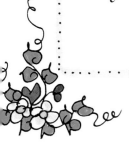

Five Tips That Make a Difference

♥ If you take out all ingredients at the beginning of a cooking project and put them away as used, the cleanup is easier and there's no doubt whether or not you have used an ingredient.

♥ Favorite recipes that you use often, whether cut from magazines or written on recipe cards, can be taped to the inside of your kitchen cabinet doors. When you're ready to cook, there's no need to rummage through clippings in envelopes or boxes. Just open your cabinet door!

♥ When shopping, don't deviate from your grocery list unless you find unadvertised sales, such as overripe fruit and day-old bakery.

♥ For those times you can't cook, prepare a small book titled "Mom's (or Dad's) Helpful Hints," in which you record easy-to-prepare recipes. Carefully note each step for every recipe and include some special cooking tips. Your family will really appreciate it.

♥ Don't forget to use your microwave, even when making a conventional recipe. Let it melt butter and chocolate, soften cheese, toast nuts, cook bacon, and thaw frozen vegetables.

When a man's stomach is full it makes no difference
whether he is rich or poor.

E u r i p i d e s

Index of Recipes